everyone's way of the cross

Clarence Enzler

Illustrated by

Annika Nelson and Gertrud Mueller Nelson

ave maria press AmP notre dame, indiana

Nihil Obstat:
John L. Reedy, C.S.C.
Censor Deputatis

Imprimatur:
Most Rev. Leo A. Pursley, D.D.
Bishop of Ft. Wayne-South Bend

Founded in 1865, Ave Maria Press is a ministry of the United States Province of Holy Cross.

www.avemariapress.com

Regular   ISBN 978-1-59471-430-6
Regular ePub ISBN 978-1-59471-455-9
Large Print   ISBN 978-1-59471-454-2
Spanish   ISBN 978-1-59471-452-8
Spanish ePub ISBN 978-1-59471-453-5

Printed and bound in the United States of America.

INTRODUCTION

Christ speaks These fourteen steps
that you are now about to walk
you do not take alone.

I walk with you.

Though you are you,
and I am I,
yet we are truly one—
one Christ.

And therefore
my way of the cross
two thousand years ago
and your "way" now
are also one.

But note this difference.
My life was incomplete until I crowned it
by my death.
Your fourteen steps
will only be complete
when you have crowned them
by your life.

JESUS IS CONDEMNED

Christ speaks In Pilate's hands, my other self,
I see my Father's will.
Though Pilate is unjust,
he has earthly power over me.

And so the Son of God obeys.

If I can bow to my Father's will,
can you also submit, even in the face of injustice?

I reply My Jesus, Lord,
obedience cost you your life.
For me
it costs an act of will—
no more—
and yet how hard it is for me to bend.

Remove the blinders from my eyes
that I may see that it is you alone whom I obey.

Lord, it is you.

Christ speaks This cross,
this chunk of tree,
is what my Father chose for me.

The crosses you must bear
are largely products of your daily life.
And yet my Father chose them, too,
for you.

Receive them from his hands.

Take heart, my other self,
I will not let your burdens grow
one ounce too heavy for your strength.

I reply My Jesus, Lord,
I take my daily cross.
I welcome the monotony
that often marks my day,
discomforts of all kinds,
the summer's heat, the winter's cold,
my disappointments, tensions, setbacks, cares.

Remind me often that
in carrying my cross,
I carry yours with you.
And though I bear a sliver only
of your cross,
You carry all of mine, except a sliver,
in return.

Christ speaks The God who made the universe,
and holds it in existence
by his will alone,
becomes a man, too weak to bear
a piece of timber's weight.

How human in his weakness is the Son of God.

My Father willed it thus.
I could not be your model otherwise.

If you would be my other self,
you also must accept without complaint
your human frailties.

I reply Lord Jesus, how can I refuse?

I willingly accept my weaknesses,
my irritations and my moods,
my headaches and fatigue,
all my defects of body, mind, and soul.

Because they are your will for me,
these "handicaps" of my humanity,
I gladly suffer them.

Make me content
with all my discontents,
but give me strength
to struggle after you.

Christ speaks My mother sees me whipped.
She sees me kicked and driven like a beast.
She counts my every wound.
But though her soul cries out in agony,
no protest or complaint
escapes her lips
or even enters her thoughts.

She shares my martyrdom—
and I share hers.
We hide no pain, no sorrow,
from each other's eyes.
This is my Father's will.

I reply My Jesus, Lord,
I know what you are telling me.
To watch the pain of those we love
is harder than to bear our own.

To carry my cross after you,
I, too, must stand and watch
the sufferings of my dear ones—
the heartaches, sicknesses, and grief
of those I love.

And I must let them watch mine, too.

I do believe—
for those who love you
all things work together unto good.

SIMON HELPS JESUS

Christ speaks My strength is gone;
I can no longer bear the cross alone.
And so the legionnaires
make Simon give me aid.

This Simon is like you, my other self.
Give me your strength.

Each time you lift some burden from another's back,
you lift as with your very hand
the cross's awful weight
that crushes me.

I reply Lord, make me realize
that every time I wipe a dish,
pick up an object off the floor,
assist a child in some small task,
or give another preference
in traffic or the store;
each time I feed the hungry,
clothe the naked,
teach the ignorant,
or lend my hand in any way—
it matters not to whom—
my name is Simon.
And the kindness I extend to them
I really give to you.

Christ speaks Can you be brave enough, my other self,
to wipe my bloody face?

Where is my face, you ask?

At home whenever eyes fill up with tears,
at work when tensions rise,
on playgrounds, in the slums,
the courts, the hospitals, the jails—
wherever suffering exists—
my face is there.
And there I look for you
to wipe away my blood and tears.

I reply Lord, what you ask is hard.
It calls for courage and self-sacrifice,
and I am weak.
Please, give me strength.
Don't let me run away because of fear.

Lord, live in me
and act in me
and love in me.
And not in me alone—in all of us—
so that we may reveal
no more your bloody but your glorious face
on earth.

Christ speaks This seventh step, my other self,
is one that tests your will.
From this fall learn to persevere
in doing good.

The time will come
when all your efforts seem to fail
and you will think,
"I can't go on."

Then turn to me,
my heavy-laden one,
and I will give you rest.

Trust me and carry on.

I reply Give me your courage, Lord.
When failure presses heavily on me
and I am desolate,
stretch out your hand
to lift me up.

I know I must not cease,
but persevere in doing good.

But help me, Lord.
Alone there's nothing I can do.
With you, I can do anything you ask.

I will.

Christ speaks How often had I longed to take
the children of Jerusalem
and gather them to me.
But they refused.

But now these women weep for me
and my heart mourns for them—
mourns for their sorrows that will come.

I comfort those who seek to solace me.

How gentle can you be, my other self?
How kind?

I reply My Jesus,
your compassion
in your passion
is beyond compare.

Lord, teach me,
help me learn.
When I would snap at those
who hurt me with their ridicule,
those who misunderstand,
or hinder me with some misguided helpfulness,
those who intrude upon my privacy—
then help me curb my tongue.

May gentleness become my cloak.

Lord, make me kind like you.

Christ speaks Completely drained of strength
I lie, collapsed, upon the cobblestones.
My body cannot move.
No blows, no kicks, can rouse it up.

And yet my will is mine.
And so is yours.

Know this, my other self,
your body may be broken,
but no force on earth and none in hell
can take away your will.

Your will is yours.

I reply My Lord,
I see you take a moment's rest
then rise and stagger on.
So I can do—
because my will is mine.

When all my strength is gone
and guilt and self-reproach
press me to earth and seem to hold me fast,
protect me from the sin of Judas—
save me from despair!

Lord, never let me feel
that any sin of mine
is greater than your love.
No matter what my past has been
I can begin anew.

Christ speaks Behold, my other self,
the poorest king who ever lived.
Before my creatures I stand stripped.
The cross—my deathbed—
even this is not my own.

Yet who has ever been so rich?

Possessing nothing, I own all—
my Father's love.

If you, too, would own everything,
be not solicitous
about your food, your clothes,
your life.

I reply My Lord,
I offer you my all—
whatever I possess,
and more, my self.

Detach me from the craving for
prestige, position, wealth.

Root out of me
all trace of envy of my neighbor
who has more than I.
Release me from the vice of pride,
my longing to exalt myself,
and lead me to the lowest place.

May I be poor in spirit, Lord,
so that I can be rich in you.

jesus is crucified

Christ speaks Can you imagine what a crucifixion is?

My executioners stretch my arms;
they hold my hand and wrist against the wood
and press the nail
until it stabs my flesh.
Then, with one heavy hammer smash,
they drive it through—
and pain
bursts like a bomb of fire in my brain.

They seize the other arm;
and agony again explodes.

Then raising up my knees
so that my feet are flat against the wood,
they hammer them fast, too.

I reply   My God,
I look at you and think:
Is my soul worth this much?

What can I give you in return?

I here and now accept
for all my life
whatever sickness, torment, agony may come.
To every cross I touch my lips.

O blessed cross that lets me be—
with you—
a co-redeemer of humanity.

Christ speaks   The cross becomes a pulpit now—
"Forgive them, Father. . . .
You will be with me in Paradise. . . .
There is your mother. . . . There . . . your son. . . .
I thirst. . . .
It is complete."

To speak I have to raise myself
by pressing on my wrists and feet,
and every move engulfs me
in new waves of agony.

And then, when I have borne enough,
have emptied my humanity,
I let my mortal life depart.

I reply   My Jesus,
God,
what can I say or do?

I offer you **my** death
with all its pains,
accepting now
the time and kind of death
in store for me.
Not by a single instant
would I lengthen my life's span.

I offer you my death
for my own sins
and for those of all humanity.

My God! My God! Forsake us not.
We know not what we do.

JESUS IS TAKEN DOWN

Christ speaks The sacrifice is done.

Yes, my Mass is complete;
but not my mother's
and not yours, my other self.

My mother still must cradle in her arms
the lifeless body of the son she bore.

You, too, must part from those you love,
and grief will come to you.

In your bereavements think of this:
A multitude of souls were saved
by Mary's sharing in my Calvary.
Your grief can also be
the price of souls.

I reply I beg you, Lord,
help me accept the partings that must come—
from friends who go away,
my children leaving home,
and most of all, my dear ones
when you shall call them to yourself.

Then, give me grace to say:
"As it has pleased you, Lord,
to take them home,
I bow to your most holy will.
And if by just one word
I might restore their lives against your will,
I would not speak."
Grant them eternal joy.

jesus is buried

Christ speaks So ends my mortal life.

But now another life begins
for Mary,
and for Magdalen,
for Peter and for John,
and you.

My life's work is done.
My work within and through my church
must now commence.

I look to you, my other self.

Day in, day out, from this time forth,
be my apostle—
victim—
saint.

I reply My Jesus, Lord,
you know my spirit is as willing
as my flesh is weak.

The teaching you could not impart,
the sufferings you could not bear,
the works of love you could not do
in your short life on earth,
let me impart,
and bear,
and do
through you.

But I am nothing, Lord.
Help me!

conclusion

Christ speaks I told you at the start, my other self,
my life was not complete
until I crowned it by my death.
Your "way" is not complete
unless you crown it by your life.

Accept each moment as it comes to you,
with faith and trust
that all that happens has my mark on it.
A simple *fiat*, this is all it takes;
a breathing in your heart,
"I will it, Lord."

So seek me not in far-off places.
I am close at hand.
Your workbench, office, kitchen,
these are altars
where you offer love.
And I am with you there.

Go now! Take up your cross
and with your life
complete your way.